IMAGES
of America

SANDWICH

Joan Bark Hardekopf
with the Sandwich Historical Society

ARCADIA
PUBLISHING

Published by Arcadia Publishing
Charleston SC, Chicago IL, Portsmouth NH, San Francisco CA

Library of Congress Catalog Card Number: 2008925892

For all general information contact Arcadia Publishing at:
Telephone 843-853-2070
Fax 843-853-0044
E-mail sales@arcadiapublishing.com
For customer service and orders:
Toll-Free 1-888-313-2665

Visit us on the Internet at www.arcadiapublishing.com

The author, Joan Bark Hardekopf, is shown at the Stone Mill Museum in Sandwich in a recent photograph.

CONTENTS

ACKNOWLEDGMENTS

Sandwich is fortunate to have several collectors of significant historical artifacts to help preserve the past. I am truly grateful for all of you who have taken the time and effort to share information and photographs to make it possible to present this book to the community.

Special thanks goes to the following people and groups for lending the photographs that appear in this book: Janice and Bill Abens, Allen Armes, June Bannister, Clare Beverage, Mike and Mary Breunig, Lori Carey, Pat Clapper, Joe Fraser, Merle and Flora Griswold, Scott Harrod, Barbara Hoffman, Susan Hohenberger, Joiner History Room, Gary Moss, Shawn Rogers, Judy Rohrer, Salem Lutheran Church, Sandwich District Library, Jeff Scull, Stone Mill Museum, Darrell Trout, Ron Wallis, and the author's collection.

Thank you to Janice Abens, Pat Clapper, Barbara Hoffman, and Judy Rohrer for spending many days in 2007 at the museum helping with research. Thank you to Karen Breunig and Vivian C. Wright for their layout and proofreading expertise and to proofreaders Janice Abens and Barbara Hoffman.

I appreciate all the help and guidance from Arcadia Publishing contacts Jeff Ruetsche and John Pearson, who were there when I had questions or concerns. And a big thank-you to my husband, Lyle, who was patient and pitched in to help when needed so I could work on the book.

A project such as this is a learning experience for everyone involved. It is my hope that you will enjoy reading and looking at the book as much as we enjoyed compiling it.

My love of doing research is one of the reasons for compiling this book. It is with great pleasure that I present it to you.

INTRODUCTION

Sandwich was not the only name considered for this community back in the mid-1850s. Other names were Almon, after an early settler, and Newark Station. Sandwich was chosen because of Congressman John Wentworth's influence with the railroad officials. The name was taken from his hometown of Sandwich, New Hampshire.

One of the earliest settlers in 1844 was Almon Gage. He gave the railroad five acres on the condition it would erect the necessary depot buildings within five years. Gage offered lots to anyone who came to erect a building. The first person to respond was James Clark. Clark built the short-lived Donegana House at the southeast corner of Main and Railroad Streets. The depot was built in 1855, two years after the completion of the railroad tracks, attracting large industry.

One of the first businesses to come was the Sandwich Manufacturing Company followed by the Sandwich Enterprise Company. Several hundred people were employed at the factories, which shipped farm implements to all parts of the world. A large brick and tile factory supplied products for farm tiling and building in the community. Bricks were also used for paving the downtown streets.

Many farms were established in the area with the soil being very black, flat, and fertile. The first farms were north of town along the Somonauk Creek. Farming is still an important part of the area now but on a different scale. The average farm size is much larger, and there are fewer farmers.

The area is rich with Native American artifacts like arrowheads, axes, and pottery. Shabbona, a Potawatomi Indian chief, roamed the area as a friend of many. Sandwich Township is actually one half of a township, being divided off from Somonauk Township in 1898 after some disagreements.

Sandwich was progressive in the early years. A power plant and city water were installed in 1883, a fire department in 1884, electric lights in 1893, telephones in 1898, and a sewer system in 1912. There were 203 families here in 1860. The population in 1910 was 2,500.

In 2008, Sandwich has about 6,500 residents in its three square miles. Although there are several small industries, a large number of residents commute to the east for employment. It is still a growing, friendly community that continues to draw new people to the area and is a good place to retire. The town is known for its Sandwich Fair, April to October antique shows, antique and unique shopping. Recently a 100-bed hotel and a convention center were completed; an indoor water park will be completed soon.

This book is a good representation of life in Sandwich from its beginning around 1853 through the 1950s. The town was established in 1859, became a city in 1872, and W. W. Sedgwick was elected the first mayor. Sandwich will be 150 years old in 2009.

—Joan Bark Hardekopf

This 1856 three-story building at 315 East Railroad Street is the Stone Mill Museum. It was deeded in 1965 by James Knights to the newly formed Sandwich Historical Society. It opened as a museum in 1969. It is open Sundays from April to October, 1:00 p.m. to 4:00 p.m., except some holidays.

One

PLACES OF WORSHIP AND
PLACES OF LEARNING

The Church of Jesus Christ of Latter-day Saints organized in Sandwich in 1859 and met on East Hall Street until 1902, when the church was deliberately burned. Then they rented the German Lutheran Church on South Main Street until they purchased the church at 109 North Castle Street (above) in 1925 for $850 from the Norwegian Lutherans. The Church of Jesus Christ of Latter-day Saints no longer meets in Sandwich. Today this is the Bread of Life Tabernacle.

A group of Baptists started gathering north of Somonauk in 1842 before moving to Sandwich in 1853, where they built the first church, the First Baptist Church, in Sandwich at the southwest corner of Main and Church Streets for $2,100. They merged with the Presbyterians in 1917. Later the church became the Pictorial Paper Package Corporation.

After worshiping at the academy at the southwest corner of Church and Wolfe Streets, the Presbyterians built the third church in Sandwich, the First Presbyterian, at the northeast corner of Eddy and First Streets. The south-facing church was dedicated in 1858. A 16-foot addition was put on in 1866. In 1892, it was changed to face the west. The Roman Catholics purchased it in 1910.

In November 1897, Sandwich was captivated by an evangelist invited to the area by several local churches. When the Sandwich Opera House became too small after the first evening of evangelist Milan B. Williams's daily services, the community built this 70-foot-by-90-foot tabernacle at the corner of Second and Green Streets (above) in 22 working hours. It seated 1,400 people and included space for a choir of 150 (below). Williams and gospel singer Charles Alexander held well-attended nightly services for a month before moving on. The building was later moved about two blocks southeast on Center Street to be used for manufacturing. It is there today just west of Main Street.

This little church has quite a history. It originally was the Chapel for the Congregational Church at Third and Eddy Streets. In 1860, it was moved to South Main Street next to the First Baptist Church and became the German Lutheran Church (pictured). In 1925, it was sold to Our Saviour's Lutheran congregation.

The Norwegian Lutheran's first service was in 1888. They met in members' homes before purchasing the 109 North Castle Street building in 1903 and changing its name soon after to Our Saviour's Lutheran. In 1925, the congregation purchased the German church on South Main Street. In 2003, the church site was sold to Walgreen's drugstore. Much of the church was dismantled and incorporated into a new church built north of Sandwich and dedicated in October 2006.

Land was purchased at 403 North Main Street by the Presbyterians. Their new building, dedicated in 1912, cost $28,000. On May 20, 1917, the Presbyterian and Baptist churches voted to unite, becoming the Federated Church. The photograph is from the 1940s before additions were made to the building.

Children and adults posed for this Sunday School Rally Day photograph at the Federated Church on October 1, 1922.

The Methodists (formerly known as the Methodist Episcopals) organized in 1836 and built the second church in Sandwich. In 1854, they built a wooden church; later it was sold, divided into two sections, and moved. This first brick structure (above), finished in 1907, cost about $12,000. It burned in 1908 just 10 months after its dedication and was rebuilt the same year on the old walls and tower, looking very similar to the 1907 structure. In 1970, the Methodists and Congregationalists merged as the United Church. The church burned on December 31, 1973, the result of arson. A new church was erected on Lions Road.

The Methodist, Federated, and Congregational churches held a joint vacation Bible school in June 1944. Pictured from left to right are (first step) Jerry Mall, Donna Barter, Robert Hanson, and Richard Serby; (second step) Ronald Schultz, Sandra Schultz, Faith Brady, Ann Kofol, Mary Walker, Barbara Kegel, James Anderson, and Harold Casner; (third step) Patricia Mall, Bonnie Butler, unidentified, Barbara Rhoads, Jerry Potter, Robert Kegel, and Janet Serby; (fourth step) teachers Pauline Newton, Merle Barter, Verian Mall, Phyllis Baie, and Izeta Hanson.

This neat little church at 117 East Second Street is home to the First Church of Christ, Scientist. The society, organized in 1953 by a small group of interested persons, purchased the building from Salem Lutheran Church in 1956.

The Chapel was the first church of the Congregationalists. It was built in 1857 at the southwest corner of Eddy and Third Streets. The German Lutherans purchased and moved it in 1860. This wooden structure replaced the Chapel in 1865 and was used until it was razed in 1910.

This attractive stone structure was built in 1910 at the same Eddy and Third Streets location for $22,500, which included the organ built during Dr. James M. Lewis's 40 years as pastor. The Apostolic Church purchased it in 1972.

The Salem Lutheran Church (formerly Swedish Evangelical Lutheran) first built a church in 1876. It was later sold to the Church of Jesus Christ of Latter-day Saints and moved to the west part of town. In 1908, they purchased the German Evangelical Church for $2,525 at 117 East Second Street and worshiped there until they sold it in 1956 to the Sandwich Christian Scientist Society. At that time, they built at the corner of Main Street and Pleasant Avenue.

The present Salem Lutheran Church at Main Street and Pleasant Avenue was built in 1956 and 1957. A 13th-century granite block came from Sweden for the cornerstone. Additions have been made, most recently in 2007.

The Catholic Diocese of Rockford bought the 110 North Eddy Street church from the Presbyterians in 1910 for $2,500. In 1925, the L wing was removed, and the church was relocated to the south side of the lot, making room for the structure's remodeling and a rectory. The church owns land north of town and hopes to build there soon. Its parish center is on Arnold Road.

The Nazarenes purchased property for their church on College and Green Streets in 1949. Members held services in the basement, which was completed in 1950. Using some of the lumber salvaged from the razed New Idea Spreader Company buildings, church members and friends donated their labor to complete the church, and it was dedicated on May 4, 1958.

The first south-side school was organized and built in 1854 as an L-shaped, two-story, two-room academy in the 100 block of West Church Street. J. T. Hendricks conducted the private school. The school district purchased it in 1856, and it remained a grammar school. In 1894, it was sold and cut into two sections. One part was moved to the southeast part of town, and the other part was moved to the west end of town for a barn. Both structures have been torn down.

W. W. Woodbury (top left), the janitor S. D. Nye (top right), and students are pictured at the grammar school in 1892. Woodbury was a longtime teacher and superintendent. Other earlier schools included an 1840 log schoolhouse west of town near the fairgrounds and an 1845 red schoolhouse at Main and Center Streets, which was used until 1857 then sold and moved to the south side of town for a dwelling.

This little building was originally located on Green Street just south of Third Street as one of the first schools in Sandwich. By 1903, it was moved to 28 West Church Street. Before its demolition in 1969, it served as a bicycle shop, meat market, restaurant, and paint store.

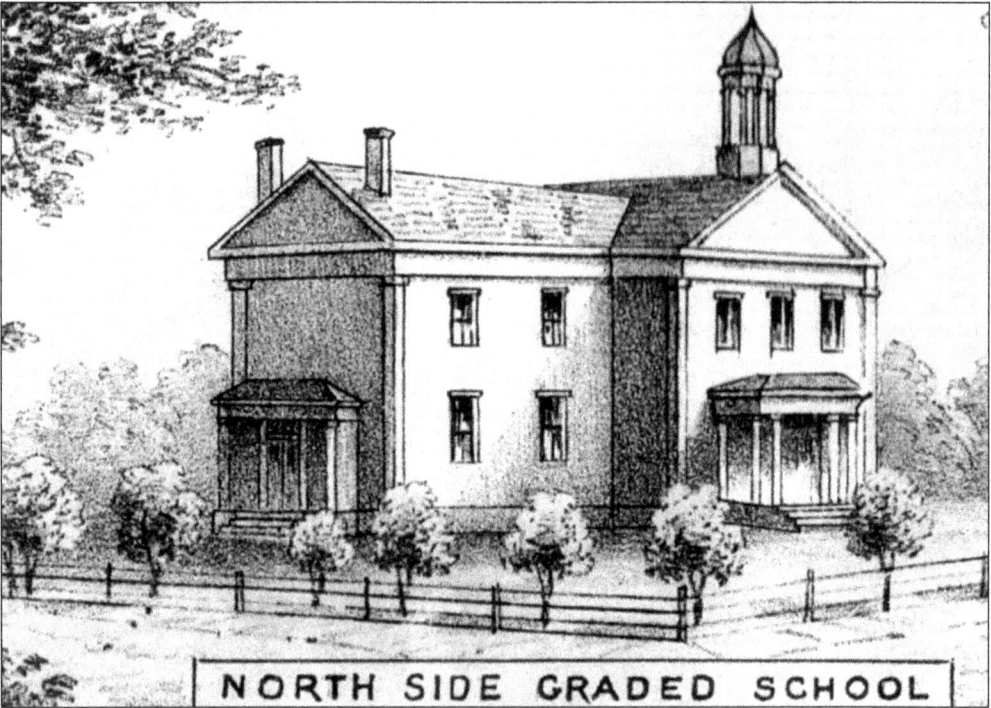

NORTH SIDE GRADED SCHOOL

In 1859, a building similar to the South Side Graded School was erected as the high school on the site now occupied by the W. W. Woodbury School on East Third Street. Small additions were made to both schools, which were under the control of a board of directors until the first board of education was elected in 1873. This building was made into two homes; one moved to Sixth Street and the other to Washington Street to make room for the new 1894 school.

The brick south side grammar school was built at 100 West Church Street in 1894 for $10,000 after a six-year debate. In 1932, it was named A. E. Woodward School, honoring the 16-year tenure of a leading politician, civic figure, and president of the school board. The school was torn down in 1967 and now is the site of Castle Bank.

The W. W. Woodbury School was built in 1894 for $12,000 and was very similar to the south side school. It faced south in the 300 block of Third Street and was used as the high school for many years and later the junior high and grade school. In 1967, it was torn down and replaced with the current grade school.

These six ladies made up the 1908 high school girls' basketball team. From left to right are (first row) Gladys Vincent, Ada Hennis, and Bess McKindley; (second row) Irene Hummel, Erma Bell, and Lucille Hummel.

From left to right, the 1908 championship northeastern Illinois baseball team includes (first row) Arthur Spickerman, Charles Haymond, Earl Lowman, Bert Spickerman, Rhea Smith, and Wilbur Hennis; (second row) coach George Schlaffer, Roy Smith, Oliver Wallace, Cedric Lewis, Arthur Becker, and Harvey Jones.

The 1911 high school football squad is pictured. From left to right are (first row) Richard Freeland, Edward Kukuk, Laird Thorpe, and Malcolm Woodward; (second row) Miles B. Castle, Wallace Cochran, Edward Meilinger, Edward Fields, Ernest Miller, Harry Darnell, and Rex Meilinger; (third row) coach W. W. Woodbury, Owen Rogers, Paul Oschida, Lloyd Faxon, and Carl Kaiser.

The 1929 men's high school varsity basketball players, from left to right, are (first row) D. Cortright, D. Rosentreter, J. Connolly, L. Woods, P. Graf, and A. Killey; (second row) D. Dean, A. Woodward, K. Erwin, R. Cooper, D. Wesson, R. McInturf, C. Creasey, B. Knights, O. Johnson, and R. Gengler; (third row) coach Elvan Wright, E. Killey, A. Puhan, F. Schrader, unidentified, C. Scent, G. Potter, L. Fanning, C. Massat, and coach Clarence Allen.

After a two-year legal battle ending in the Illinois Supreme Court, this brick building on South Wells Street was constructed in 1921 and 1922 on 15 acres as the high school. There was an addition in 1954 and a renovation in 2002. In 1966, it became the Herman Dummer Junior High School and now houses the fourth and fifth grades. Dummer was a longtime school administrator, alderman, and police magistrate.

These students were chosen for safety patrol crossing guard duty in 1946 for busy Route 34. The program was sponsored by the Chicago Motor Club. Pictured from left to right are (first row) Donald Potter, Sidney Allen, Jerry Mall, and Ronald Carr; (second row) Joyce Kinchner, Beverly Hupach, Carol Houghtby, Theresa Fields, Janet Becendorf, Susan Scheidecker, Patricia Jensen, Lucille Schoener, and Patricia Titzel; (third row) Merle Eide, Ronald Wallis, Bruce Walley, Ralph Bennett, James Wilhelm, R. Latham, Charles Strode, John McQuown, Warren Westbrook, and Dale Dierzen.

The 1958 varsity basketball team broke the record for the number of wins. Pictured from left to right are (first row) James Leasure and James Gord; (second row) Charles Naylon, Wendell Smith, David Dwyer, Jerry Casner, James Hill, and Jon Eriksson; (third row) coach Harold Erickson, James Fish, LaVerne Wilkening, George Lindner, Douglas Abraham, James Bernhardt, and coach Richard Giles.

The Lynn G. Haskin School at 720 South Wells Street was erected between 1954 and 1956. It was also named after a long-serving teacher and superintendent of schools and is presently a grade school. Other schools built later were Prairie View, Indian Valley Vocational, and the middle school.

These are the "can-can girls" from the French Club in the 1960 homecoming parade. Their float's theme was "We can-can win." Shown in the photograph from left to right are Janet Hough, Karen Hardersen, Pamela White, Jeanne Steffen, Patricia Casson, Sharon Byro, Sharon Porter Schleuker, LeAnn Scheidecker, Joanne Martin, and Helle Nielsen.

Located on 58 acres on Lions Road, Sandwich High School was dedicated on April 23, 1967, with an initial capacity of 450 pupils. With its additions, it remains the high school today, but a new high school is in the planning stage.

26

Two

WARTIME

James Westbury Tanser was born in England in July 1852. He came to America in 1876 and became a naturalized citizen. He served at Fort Clark and Fort Worth in the Indian Wars, being honorably discharged November 1886. He was the only known area soldier who served in the Indian Wars.

A company of 112 men called Sandwich Union Guards was organized, uniformed by the women, and on its way to Cairo, Illinois, within a week of the April 1861 call from Pres. Abraham Lincoln. This 10th regiment was led by Lindsay Carr (pictured), who was killed by a bullet from a rebel sharpshooter. Soon after, another company, the Sandwich Rifles led by Fred Partridge, was sent from the Sandwich area.

Organized by 33 women on May 28, 1891, the Sandwich Women's Relief Corps 182 was the women's group of the Grand Army of the Republic (GAR). The group was still active in 1953. Part of its charitable work included executing the plans made by the GAR for Memorial Day activities. The ladies not only made local contributions, but they also sent offerings of fruits, jellies, and bedding to soldiers' and soldiers widows' homes.

Oak Ridge Cemetery is on the west edge of Sandwich. In the center of the cemetery, a cannon stands proudly as a memorial to GAR Post 510. It was obtained by the Sandwich Women's Relief Corps in 1904. A plaque on one side reads, "Sandwich WRC to Post 510 GAR." The other side reads, "To Our Nation's Heroes 1904."

Sandwich had a fife and drum corps, which was formed in 1861 as the Asbury Martial Band at the establishment of Company H of the 105th Illinois Infantry for the Civil War.

The GAR Post 510 was composed of men who served in the Civil War from 1861 to 1865 as an organization to support and assist each other. It was a popular group and marched in many parades. The post dissolved in September 1926. There were seven members at that time but not enough to fill the officer positions.

Pictured is a typical parade in Sandwich. The 1897 Fourth of July parade was routed along Railroad Street. Participants included decorated carriages, floats, the Union Band, the GAR Post 510, the fire department, the mayor and councils, teachers, clergy, and the board of education.

The Sandwich Red Cross chapter from World War I held a high place in the state in all branches of war work. Several townships in southern DeKalb County were admitted to membership in the Sandwich chapter.

Victory Day in Sandwich on November 11, 1918, was the day local citizens celebrated the official end to World War I after the armistice was signed. After World War II, the official name was changed to Veterans Day. Dr. George S. Culver dressed as Uncle Sam for the float in this parade. Impromptu parades were held all over town.

The Union Band participated in the November 11, 1918, parade. They are shown on South Main Street at Church Street. An annual celebration was held for several years after 1918 on November 11 with taps and the firing of guns, ending the day with a banquet and a speaker. The 1928 banquet tickets at the Congregational Church cost 75¢.

It was a cold, frosty day on Monday, November 11, 1918, and the end of World War I was a wild and noisy time in Sandwich. People were reluctant to believe the news, as there had been a fake report the previous week. Church bells rang and whistles blew during the day while people gathered. A victory dinner was held soon after the celebration. The gazebo, pictured above, was constructed for the celebration.

32

Prominent citizens of Sandwich, calling themselves Entre Nous, portrayed various roles at the November 11, 1918, parade and celebration. The members, from left to right, are (first row) N. Wallace, M. Houston, M. Castle, Dr. George S. Culver, Dr. Louise Culver, D. Converse, J. Mosher, A. Prescott, L. Stinson, W. Prescott, M. Woodward, and A. Woodward; (second row) E. Mosher, C. Warner, J. Wallace, B. Howison, G. Latham, Ira Converse, C. Stinson, W. Wallace, A. Hamill, M. Wallace, I. Wallace, and J. Latham.

All branches of the military gathered near the Sandwich City Hall/Opera House for a World War I homecoming photograph on October 10, 1919.

In 1942, this display of area servicemen and women was in the window at Hornsby's store. Gold Star boys (killed in action) included Reed V. Larson and Harry D. Miller of the army air force, Glenn A. Morris and Harry J. Riis of the army, and William D. Schultz of the navy air corps.

Students joined the World War II efforts by collecting old newspapers and scrap iron. They are shown here filling Louis Mall's truck.

Three

COMMUNITY EVENTS

Hog Day, a special event, was held in Sandwich in 1892. Farmers brought wagons full of hogs on their way to the freight depot. The Sandwich City Hall/Opera House is in the left background.

This original fair poster is at the Stone Mill Museum. Prior to the Sandwich Fair, an agricultural event was sponsored by the Union Agricultural Institute starting in 1858. Tickets in 1873 were 25¢; children under 12 were 15¢. The fair has ranged from two to five days long and has been continuous since 1888, even through the Great Depression.

The little, red, round office at the Sandwich Fair is believed to date back to 1891. Originally it was the judges' stand, located on the racetrack. Later it was moved near its present location and served as a bandstand. It was shortened three to four feet and remodeled in the 1960s. Today it is the concession and vendor office located in the center of the fairgrounds.

In 1892, this two-story barnlike structure was the 100-foot-by-150-foot floral hall at the Sandwich Fair. It housed fruit, grain, vegetables, floral exhibits, work from public school children, fancy work, and merchandise from local businesses. Lightning struck and destroyed it in May 1905. A new industrial hall replaced the building for the 1905 fair. Today the well-known landmark is called the home arts building and displays food and needlework during the fair.

The original horticulture building at the Sandwich fairgrounds was built for $2,000 in 1905. A large addition was added in 1915. Although a fire destroyed the building in 1931, a similar building was rebuilt in time for the 1931 fair.

Chautauquas were held in large tents at the Sandwich fairgrounds from 1906 to 1921. They were generally 10-day events with outstanding lecturers and musicians. Speakers included William Jennings Bryan and Rev. W. A. (Billie) Sunday. Topics were educational, religious, and entertaining. They left a great imprint on the social and cultural life of rural communities like Sandwich. Tents could be rented on the grounds for overnight stays. Season tickets were 50¢ and $1, and families were encouraged to attend. There were programs for all ages, including cooking schools and moving pictures. A 1923 five-day Chautauqua was held near Third and Green Streets.

In 1902, the fire department sponsored a corn carnival and street fair for three days. In keeping with the theme, nearly every business in town had a display of corn. Carnival rides and games lined the streets. Vendors sold their wares, which included souvenirs of the occasion. This photograph is looking west on Railroad Street. The City Hotel was just west of the Sandwich City Hall/Opera House.

The Parade of Progress took place on August 25, 1950, in downtown Sandwich. It was a celebration in recognition of the Railroad Street widening and new lighting in the business district. An estimated 3,000 people watched as more than 50 floats and entries extended for a mile along the route. The early lives of Native Americans through the 1950s were portrayed.

A truck transported the memorial cannon from the Rock Island Ordinance Depot to Sandwich. It was placed in the city park on August 25, 1934, with the original coat of camouflaged war paint but without the firing mechanism and instruments. It came from the German war-torn fields of the western front.

Hundreds of people came to observe the 1934 dedication of the cannon in memory of World War I veterans. The Sandwich Veterans of Foreign Wars (VFW) Post 1486 obtained the cannon from the government. The cannon was moved to the VFW grounds on South Main Street when the park became a parking lot.

In 1938, Easter Sunday was broadcast nationwide by NBC radio from a North Main Street parade in Sandwich. Sandwich was selected because of the publisher of the *Sandwich Free Press*, Hedwig Easter. The actual broadcast was only five minutes long. Pictured from left to right are Helen Cochran, Mayor Wallace Cochran, Edward Easter, NBC announcer David Zimmerman, and Hedwig Easter.

Oatman Brothers Dairy sponsored a float in a 1950 local parade promoting its products. On the float, from left to right, are Beverly Tuttle, Patricia Mall, Barbara Rhoads, Lorraine DeGroot, Patricia Nelson, Sharon Lett, and Lowell "Rusty" Phillips.

Jane Werner is shown here trimming Elmer Johnson's beard for competition judging during the 1959 centennial. Men's groups were part of Brothers of the Brush; women's groups were part of Sisters of the Swish.

In 1959, Sandwich celebrated its centennial. Residents participated by growing beards, moustaches, not wearing makeup, and dressing in period clothing. These employees of RV Pump, manufacturer of vacuum pumps for Surge milking machines, pose outside of their workplace on West Church Street.

Four

TRAINS AND INDUSTRY

A petition to establish a railroad station at Sandwich was presented in 1853. This wooden depot was built in 1855 at 202 East Center Street, two years after the tracks from Aurora to Mendota were completed. The depot was sold in 1913, split in two, and moved to Latham Street for residences.

A freight office was built in 1860, seven years after the tracks from Aurora to Mendota were completed and five years after Sandwich's first depot was built on the north side of East Railroad Street. A large fenced-in pen at the east end of the building held livestock until the train or local farmers picked them up. The structure was razed in 1973 for a city building.

In the late 1880s, a freight train thundering through downtown Sandwich was a common sight. Looking west from Eddy Street, one can see the Kehl Brothers building on the right and the Marcy Block on the left.

A watchman tower stood on the north side of the railroad tracks at the Main Street railroad crossing. On December 25, 1947, the gatekeeper, Edward Schumaker, was in the tower when a derailed freight car bumped into the tower, knocking it down. Schumaker received lifelong injuries from the accident.

This 100-foot brick passenger depot was built in 1913, replacing the wooden structure. It was a spacious 2,640-square-foot building that was well used for many years. Two passenger trains stopped here in early 1971, but soon after, no trains stopped. It was demolished in 1985 despite efforts by local citizens to save the building.

A three-story stone building stands proudly at the corner of Railroad and Lafayette Streets. The Stone Mill was built in 1856 as a working steam gristmill. It closed in 1892 because of faltering business. It was then used for manufacturing farm equipment parts and by James Knights, until Knights deeded it to the historical society in 1965.

Employees of the steam gristmill took a break to have their photograph taken in 1891. The mill had a capacity of 100 barrels of flour per day. It was said to have been one of the best mills in the state. The first miller received a portion of the finished flour as his pay. Early names for the business included Sandwich Steam Grist Mill, Sandwich Milling, Eclipse Mill, Exchange Mill, Sandwich Roller Mill, and Eureka Roller Flouring Mill.

Just west of the fairgrounds was a brick and tile works that started in 1858. A good supply of clay was available for farm tiling, a new idea that was in great demand. The brick business was also very good, making over 800,000 bricks a year by hand. About 1890, the supply of good clay ran out, demand diminished, and the business closed. The original barn, which was the drying shed, is all that remains. In the early years, the business was called Emmons and McCoy, later it was called Dieterich and Ebinger.

Augustus Adams started a small machine shop in 1856 that led to the Sandwich Manufacturing Company, which employed up to 400 people. The plant covered about three city blocks north of Center Street on Main Street. It manufactured corn shellers, gas engines, hay presses, loaders, rakes, and grain elevators. It was sold in 1930 to the New Idea Spreader Company.

In May 1899, the Clean Sweep Special was composed of 39 railroad cars loaded with 810 Clean Sweep hay loaders made at Sandwich Manufacturing Company, each weighing 985 pounds. The cars headed west. At Creston, Iowa, the cars were divided and sent to western Iowa and South Dakota. Banners on the railcar sides told of the contents, and two brooms on the engine represented the name Clean Sweep.

Early manufacturing companies gave Sandwich its solidity and wealth and furnished steady employment to many of its citizens. Pictured in this 1907 photograph are Sandwich Manufacturing Company workers. In this photograph are Samuel Mitten, John Van Winkle, Hugh Carner, William Losee, James Hinton, Benjamin Chambers, Jonathon Mead, John Ledoyt, Fred Zimwerlee, and Lewis Greenwood.

Kennedy Brothers started the Sandwich Enterprise Company (above) in 1868 on Main Street across from the Sandwich Manufacturing Company. It extended east to Eddy Street. Sandwich Enterprise specialized in windmills but also made farm implements, feed mills, cultivators, pumps, and planters. The four-story building in the background was built in 1872 and was demolished in 1935. It was sold in 1913 to Sandwich Manufacturing Company after going through financial problems and closing a couple of times. The Otto Grain Elevator and Wagon Dump (below) were featured in a 1905 advertisement for the Sandwich Enterprise Company. August Otto of Sandwich invented these farm implements as well as a hay loader, which were helpful at harvest time for farmers who stored grain.

At the southeast corner of Main and Center Streets stood this three-story, 30-foot-by-120-foot building. It was erected in the late 1800s. Henry and John Kehl manufactured carriages, buggies, and wagons here in the 1880s and 1890s. The third floor was removed in 1965, and the building was torn down in 1983 to make way for a parking lot. Bricks were used to patch the Sandwich Opera House.

Gustav Walters was a blacksmith, horseshoer, and manufacturer of carriages and wagons. His specialty was road carts. This building at the northwest corner of Main and Church Streets was new in 1891, and the upper floor was used as a showroom. Walters was in business in Sandwich from 1876 to 1910.

Sandwich Creamery at 308 East College Street won the Illinois Dairymen's grand sweepstakes award for its butter in the early 1900s. The business started in 1871 as the Sandwich Cheese Factory and ended as Oatman Brothers Dairy, closing in 1961. The wooden building burned in 1910 but was rebuilt as the two-story cement block building pictured above.

Oatman Brothers purchased the dairy in 1919 to make condensed milk. Their employees at the Sandwich plant are pictured in 1946. The business closed in 1961, and the school district purchased the property in 1970. The city bought and remodeled one building to use as the police station.

The New Idea Spreader Company of Coldwater, Ohio, purchased the Sandwich Manufacturing Company in 1930. It manufactured farm implements much the same as Sandwich Manufacturing Company. The Sandwich factory closed in 1955, and the warehouse closed in 1981.

This September 1938 photograph is of employees in the forge shop and punch press department at the New Idea Spreader Company. Their well-known products were elevators, manure spreaders, and hay and corn harvesting equipment.

Century Manufacturing Company, known as the "overall factory," was located in the Hummel building at the northwest corner of Main and Center Streets. It opened in 1932 and continued making work clothing using the Sandy All brand until 1981. The local merchants helped bring them to Sandwich and paid the building rent for at least a year. They made clothing for men, women, and children.

In 1918, Pictorial Paper Package Corporation leased the old Baptist church at the southwest corner of Main and Church Streets and made it into a factory to produce boxes, cartons, and labels. They also had a factory in Aurora. The building was razed in 1935 for a gas and service station.

James Knights and Leon Faber founded the James Knights Company in March 1942 at the request of the federal government. They produced quartz crystals used in wartime radio communications equipment. For many years, it was the largest industry in Sandwich. It was first located at the corner of Church and Wells Streets.

This is a group photograph of workers at the downtown James Knights factory prior to its June 1974 move to Reimann Avenue. The company merged with CTS (Chicago Telephone Supply) Corporation of Elkhart, Indiana, in 1964 and closed in Sandwich in 2002.

Five

BUSINESSES

George Kleinsmid's hardware store occupied the corner of Main and Railroad Streets from about 1865 to 1900. This photograph was taken on Decoration Day in 1899. This was also the earlier site of one of the first buildings in town, the Donegana House, part hotel and part store, which was built by James Clark.

George B. Hollenback was one of the early dry goods merchants at the southeast corner of Main and Railroad Streets from about 1857 to 1865. He also handled groceries, glassware, boots, shoes, ready-made clothing, furniture, and coffins. An 1859 advertisement announced the business was introducing a "ready pay system," or goods could be purchased on credit. The west half of the store was occupied by S. D. and L. S. Humiston, dry goods merchants.

Continuing east on Railroad Street from right to left are the C. D. Gaddis clothing and tailor shop; Patton and Culver's general merchandise, flour, and feed store; George P. Hay's tailor and clothing business; and Amos B. Shepard's dry goods store

A disastrous fire occurred in February 1893 at the Marcy Block on the corner of South Main and Railroad Streets. The north building of three wooden structures was destroyed and other buildings were heavily damaged. The remaining two buildings were moved to the corner of Second and Lafayette Streets and made into an apartment house.

The north store of the building adjacent to the railroad tracks on Main Street that burned in the 1893 fire included this cigar factory and Irve Schrader's barbershop. Thomas D. Emerson bought the cigar store in 1884 when he first came to Sandwich. He reopened the store in the new Marcy Block building. Schrader moved to the opposite corner above Kleinsmid's hardware store and then to other locations.

Dr. Charles Winne (left) served in the Civil War as a surgeon and upon returning home became a partner to Theron Potter in a drugstore business on East Railroad Street. In 1888, he bought out Potter and added his son-in-law Ira Converse (right). Winne was involved in the business until 1903.

Bothered with health problems, Converse took Fred Smith as a partner in his East Railroad Street drugstore. Smith retired in 1912, but Converse remained in business until he retired in 1926 and sold it to Richard Holland. Pictured in 1905, from left to right, are Converse, an unidentified salesman, and Beulah and Robert A. Woodward, jeweler.

Charles Gage and Frank McKindley started the Gage and McKindley grocery store in 1885 at 44 East Railroad Street. There was some renumbering of addresses, as the earlier address was 11 East Railroad Street. In 1893, Gage retired, but McKindley continued.

McKindley Grocery on East Railroad Street was advertised as "eight steps from the Post Office." Hugh N. McKindley purchased the business in 1874, sold it later, and then his son Frank returned to the business in 1885. It was sold in 1940 to R. E. Page and Son's Grocery and later to Harold Hanson for a grocery store. Today it is Sandwich Office Supply.

Railroad Street between Main and Eddy Streets in the late 1890s or early 1900s showed these businesses, from left to right, the Independent Order of Odd Fellows (IOOF) building, McKindley's Grocery, Corlinsky's dry goods, and Newton Drug Store, which offered drugs, clocks, a jeweler, and an optician. The IOOF first occupied the upper floors of the building in 1860. Apartments are now on the upper floors.

Charles Corlinsky was a dry goods merchant from the 1870s at various locations in downtown Sandwich. In the late 1800s, he was at this Railroad Street location, and at times he also ran a store in Plano. He sold the business in 1909 after moving to Michigan.

Enos Doan owned a lumber and coal business from the mid-1870s to 1908. He was located at the northeast corner of Main and Railroad Streets in 1908 when he sold the business to Philip S. Lindner. Lindner also purchased the Mosher and Castle lumber and coal business in 1918. This building was moved a block west in 1920 to make way for a city park. The building was used by P. S. Lindner and Company until it closed in 2005.

This shows the interior of the 1911 P. S. Lindner and Company coal and lumber office. Pictured from left to right are Byron Lynds, Fay Harrington, Henry Severy, Fred Pratt, Philip S. Lindner, and Thomas Mercer.

At the southwest corner of Main and Center Streets this building was long known as a hotel. Built in 1853 as the two-story Emmons House, the hotel expanded in 1855 with a third story. By 1878, it was the Commercial Hotel. The third floor was the town hall and social center for several years.

Edward Thompson operated a grocery store on the street level of the Emmons Hotel, the predecessor of the Wallace House. His son Louis joined the business in 1893 and continued in the grocery business for a few years at this and other locations around Sandwich. Pictured are Louis Thompson and Anolda Kleinprinz in the 1920s.

Brothers George and Erve Wallace conducted a grocery, fruit, and chinaware business on East Railroad Street in the early 1890s. In 1894, they moved into the new Wallace Block near the same location.

The brick building at the southeast corner of Wells and Railroad Streets has a distinctive peaked corner. The Paul W. Wallace and Sons building was completed in December 1892. Businesses were on the first floor, and offices were on the second floor. This photograph was taken in 1905.

Albert Ryther was known as the "moving" man in the early days. Here he prepares to move a 14-ton boiler in 1909. He also moved buildings in the late 1890s and early 1900s. In the background is the old wooden depot.

For 20 years Albert Stevens sold coal, cement, paint, and bricks at 404 East Railroad Street. He purchased the business in 1909 from Armstrong and Newton and sold it in 1929 to A. J. Whitfield.

At Warner's Cash Store, customers bought groceries, clothing, shoes, dry goods, and more. There were several shops inside the store, similar to the shopping malls of today. James Warner started the business in 1859 and kept expanding and moving until the store filled three buildings at 3 East Railroad Street, then owned by his son James. It was advertised as "the Big Store." Warner's followed George Kleinsmid's hardware at this location.

The three-story brick building at the northwest corner of Main and Center Streets was built in 1881 by Julius M. Hummel for his farm implement, carriage, and musical instrument sales. His business was on the first floor, a billiard hall was on the second floor, and a roller rink (later a dance hall) was on the third floor. Hummel's newspaper advertisements were entertaining, as was he on his "phiddle," as he called his fiddle.

h Religion and Independent in Politics." TERMS: Per Year, if paid in Advance, $1.00. If not paid in Advance, 1.50

Newspapers published in Sandwich go back to 1857, beginning with *People's Press* and followed by the *Prairie Home Advertiser*. Both papers lasted only six months. Next came *Sandwich News*, *Sandwich Gazette*, *Sandwich Free Press*, *Sandwich Argus*, *Semi-Weekly Journal*, and *Evening Herald*. For many years the *Sandwich Argus* had these drawings that show several city buildings across the top of the front page. The *Sandwich Argus* was owned and published by Miles B. Castle, a local banker and businessman.

The three-story City Hotel was on Railroad Street where the city hall annex is today. It was also called the Park House, Hotel Egan, and Hunter Hotel. In 1916, Frank and Emory Stockham bought it, tore it down, and built a garage. Later Sandwich Motors sold Ford vehicles here; it then became French's Hardware, and now it is the city hall annex.

David Jaffe was a junk, fur, hide, and wool dealer at South East Street (now Terry Street). Jaffe started at this location in 1916 and purchased the property a few years later. In November 1943, the warehouse burned, and he built this new brick warehouse the following year. Later Jaffe's Junk and Salvage Barn was located across the street at 404 East Railroad. The Jaffe home is now Beverage Funeral Home, and the brick warehouse now houses businesses.

Jacob Burkhart started a furniture and undertaking business in 1856 with David Nixon at 127–131 South Main Street. He soon was the sole owner. In early days, the caskets were made by the undertaker. Fire destroyed the first building. It was replaced by this two-story brick structure in 1895. They closed out the furniture business and moved the funeral home to Wolfe Street in 1925, then to North Main Street, and later to Arnold Road. The business was family operated until 2003.

The Wallace House, owned by A. D. Wallace, followed the Commercial Hotel at 1 South Main Street from about 1885 to 1919. Successions of grocery stores were on the first floor as well as the post office in about 1882. Fred Harrod came to Sandwich in 1893 and purchased the grocery business in 1901 from R. C. Coy.

Harrod used this horse and delivery wagon for his business. Harrod was known for his "Phone for Food" advertisements in the newspaper.

Harrod built and moved into this building at 2 North Main Street in 1920. He sold the business to brothers George, Clarence, and Harry Ugland in 1929 and went into the insurance business. Harrod was mayor for two terms and a justice of the peace.

The Ugland brothers purchased Harrod's grocery store at the northeast corner of Main and Center Streets in 1929. Soon after, George sold his share to Harry. The grocery store closed in 1955. Pictured are Harry (left) and Clarence at their store.

Looking east on Center Street from Main Street about 1908 are the Glessner and Company bakery, a barbershop, and the Sandwich House. Henry and Arthur Glessner were the proprietors of the wholesale and retail bakery for a short time beginning in 1907. Henry was also a barber and carpenter.

William Eddy constructed this two-story hotel at 17 East Center Street in 1854 and named it Able House. Joseph and Mary Dyas, longtime owners, added a third story and large porch after they took over in 1866. They renamed it Sandwich House. Dyas was well known for serving 25¢ Sunday chicken dinners. The building was torn down in 1933.

Prior to Frank N. King entering the monument business, he had a feed and livery stable. In 1910, he bought the business at the southeast corner of Center and Green Streets from Frank Poust. Sandwich Manufacturing Company purchased the building in 1920. Later this was an early site of the library and was completely destroyed by fire in 1940.

A grain elevator has been at the west end of Railroad Street since 1912. This 1916 photograph shows the farmers' elevator, a 36-foot-square-by-74-foot-high building that had a 35,000 bushel capacity. It burned in 1950 and again 1956 when it was known as Westbrook Grain. It was rebuilt and serves the needs of area farmers today as the Elburn Co-op Sandwich Division.

Silas D. Newton continued the Armstrong and Newton monument business as sole owner in 1909. He sold the business to Frank N. King in 1920. Newton was mayor twice, an alderman, a fair director, and a member of the board of education.

F. N. King and Sons Monuments is the oldest family-owned business in Sandwich, beginning in 1920. A rear addition expanded the building in 1938. The fourth and fifth generations of the family now own the business on East Center Street. Frank was the original owner, then brothers Russell and Charles King took over, and now William and Linda King and their son Nathan run it.

Dickerman and Company operated a drugstore in the Marcy Block building (above). It opened in 1900 and added a soda fountain the following year. It was not long until it expanded. In 1913, the business was sold to R. G. Rosenstone. Holland's Drug Store (below) bought out Ira Converse's Drug Store in 1926 and moved to this location in 1946. Holland's expanded to cover the entire first floor and remained in this location until 1968, when it moved to the Indian Springs Shopping Center.

Charles K. Wertz purchased the Wallace House in 1919 for $8,000. It was the Hotel Wertz (above) until it was sold in 1945 to Perry Morris. Later it became the Fairway Hotel. The Fairway Grill opened in the basement. The Fairway Inn (below) was located on the first floor. Pictured behind the bar are Arnold Christensen (left) and Morris. The Morris family sold it in 1968 to James Wilhelm. The building has not operated as a hotel for some time. It is now the Club Sandwich.

Meyer Werner and his father-in-law, B. Wienman, established a wool, fur, and hide business in Sandwich on East Church Street in 1917. They also bought and sold junk metal. Later Werner changed the business into a gas station and sold automotive parts, and his son George joined the business.

George and Jane Werner continued the automotive parts business, M. Werner and Sons, with their son Tom taking over in 1971. Pictured in this 1940s photograph from left to right are unidentified, Jane, and George. The business was sold in 1999.

Joseph Francis owned a coal yard on West Railroad Street. He and a partner bought the business in 1893. He quit hauling coal in 1920 when there was less demand for it. His advertisements stated he was in the coal and transfer business for 38 years. His son Robert J. Francis followed in the business.

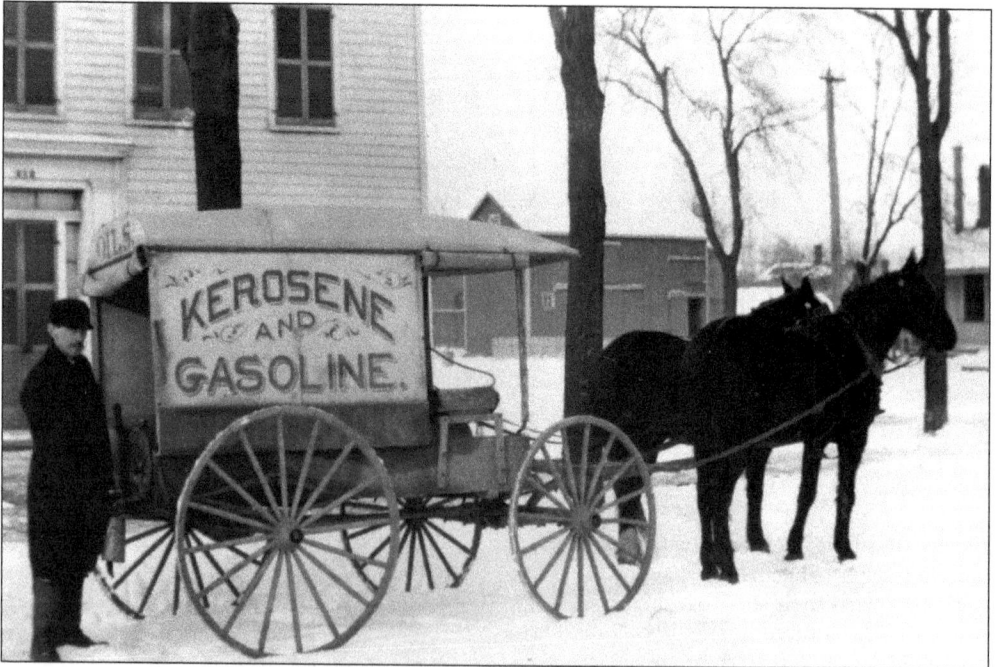

Edgar D. Brooks delivered kerosene, gasoline, and oils in this wagon in the 1890s. Brooks purchased the business from F. G. Rice in 1895 and sold it in 1899.

George W. Kleinprinz began business at the northwest corner of Eddy and Center Streets servicing and selling Overland, Dodge, and Willys cars. Pictured in 1920 at that location from left to right are Edward Martin, Sadie Kleinprinz, Samuel Bellendorf, and Jack Toombs. In November 1925, the business moved to its new building at the northeast corner of Wells and Church Streets.

Walter Nelson, automobile dealer, owned the cement block building at the southwest corner of Church and Wells Streets. In the 1920s he sold Fords, later changing to Oldsmobiles and Chevrolets. From the late 1960s to 2005, McCaslin's Bakery occupied the building.

Augustus B. Henry came to Sandwich in 1916 and bought out a branch of the Sandwich Creamery to make ice cream, locating first at an East Center Street building. In 1919, he purchased this location at 222 East Railroad Street. He and his family are shown in this 1930 photograph at the Railroad Street plant. Henry sold the business in 1945.

This is one of five ice-cream delivery trucks owned by Henry. Henry delivered ice cream in boxes and cans to retailers in 39 surrounding towns. Oatman Brothers Dairy supplied the cream. Despite the loss of an arm when he was 12 years old, Henry started making ice cream in Chicago as a young man.

In 1930, John and Randa Duvick started the Sandwich Cash Grocery at 425–427 East Railroad Street as a neighborhood grocery. This 1930s photograph shows the Duvick home (right) and their store (left). Their son James joined the business in 1936. He later renamed it Duvick's A. G. Cash Grocery and Market. In 1949, the store was sold to Howard Wilhelm.

Spickerman's home and greenhouse were at the southeast corner of Main and Church Streets. Francis Spickerman ran the greenhouse until about 1925 and then moved to California. By 1939, the greenhouse, Sandwich Floral Shop, was owned and run by Jack and Francis Toombs. The first home on this property was built in 1879 by Almon Gage. The home shown here was built in 1902; it is now part of Kelly's Pub and American Grill. The small building on the right is still a greenhouse called Sandwich Floral Shop.

Clarence Carr registered as a barber in 1919 upon returning from World War I. He bought his first shop in 1923 from Sherman Bailey. After a couple of moves, he settled at 140 South Main Street and remained there until he retired in 1949. With dimes he saved from the barbershop, Carr purchased a new Chevrolet from Nelson Motors in 1946. Carr is pictured giving a haircut to his daughter Darlene (Bastian). This area is now a parking lot.

Variety stores were a longtime business at the southeast corner of Main and Railroad Streets. Hornsby's 5¢ to $1.00 Store, owned by Mr. and Mrs. L. E. Hornsby, was there from 1933 to 1959. Lenhart's followed, owned by William Lenhart from 1959 to 1965, and then Loy's, owned by Robert Loy, was open until early 1987.

George Wahlgren (right) opened a men's clothing business in 1919 at 40 East Railroad Street when he purchased the business from Killey and Lamberson. He took Harry Darnell (left) as a partner in 1923. The Wahlgren and Darnell partnership thrived for 36 years until they retired and sold to Fred Kinchner in 1959.

Alta Oehlers started working in the millinery and women's apparel business in 1921 at Warner's Store. By 1937, she owned her own store at 127 South Main Street. Addie and Earl Olson purchased the business in 1963 and renamed it Olson's Ladies Wear. Addie operated the store until she passed away at age 90 in 1995. Fire destroyed the building in February 1998.

Glenn "Ole" Wilson started Wilson's Poultry Farm in 1925. In late 1932, he opened this new hatchery east of town, as well as a downtown Main Street location. About 90,000 chicks were hatched each week in the spring of 1935. The chicks were delivered in special boxes for miles in all directions. This building still stands at 1125 East Railroad Street.

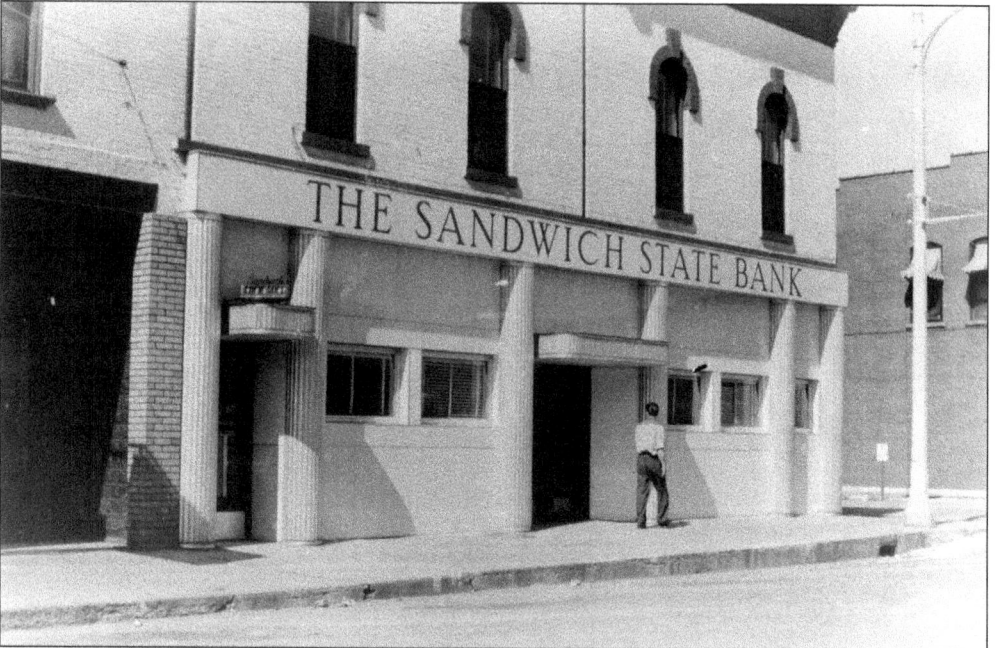

Miles B. Castle began in the banking business in Sandwich in 1856 at the northeast corner of Main and Railroad Streets. That evolved into the Sandwich State Bank at the southwest corner of Main and Railroad Streets. In 1969, the bank moved to its new facility at 100 West Church Street and is now named Castle Bank. Although the Castle family is still involved with the bank, it is owned by a larger out-of-state bank.

Floyd Sebby operated Sebby's Cash Market on the east side of Main Street just north of Church Street. He bought out his father, O. A. Sebby, in 1933 and later relocated to Center Street. The site is now a parking lot.

A gas station operated out of this tiny, brick building located on the original Route 34 near Latham and Church Streets. Later Route 34 (Church Street) was relocated slightly south of the station. Sam Browne owned the station in the 1930s. In the 1950s, it was converted to a pizza place called the Music Box Drive-In. It no longer exists.

Alois "Dutch" Reymann owned this barrel-shaped food stand, the Root Beer Barrel, in the 1930s. Originally it was located near Latham and Railroad Streets with Mr. and Mrs. Arthur Long as managers. In the 1950s, the business was moved to West Church Street and was a popular summertime eating spot. It was demolished in the mid-1960s to make room for an auction building.

Herbert Johnson built this restaurant in 1941 at 400 East Church Street and named it after his only daughter, Mary Ann. The business motto was "We Freeze to Please." It was especially popular with high school students on their way home from school. The Johnsons sold it in 1947, and it continued until about 1970. It is now a Subway restaurant.

This 75-foot railroad car was built in 1893 for the World's Columbian Exposition at a cost of $25,000. It is believed to have been used for Theodore Roosevelt's 1900 and 1904 presidential campaigns. It was retired in 1931, purchased by Henry Tattersal of Sandwich for $75, and moved in 1934 to the southwest corner of Main and Church Streets for a restaurant named the Diner. A year later, it was moved east across the street to its present location. It has also been called Wright's Diner, Paul's Diner, and Cucina Plata. Today it is Kelly's Pub and American Grill.

The Tastee-Freez on the corner of East Church and Latham Streets was a popular summertime spot for soft-serve ice cream. Toby and Maryette Wrigley built it in 1953. Other owners included Russell and June Bannister, Dean and Ethel Bagg, Max Bagg, and Lois Burkhart. Today it is Johnny K's restaurant.

In 1948, Wesley Scents and Arthur Anderson built an eight-lane bowling alley, Idle Hour Lanes, in the 900 block of East Railroad Street. Scents (pictured at left in 1948) soon became the sole owner. Today Idle Hour Lanes is owned and operated by Scents's daughter and her husband, Bonnie and Ronnie Miller.

Carl and Merle Griswold owned Griswold's Feed and Supply at 211 East Railroad Street from 1952 to 1960. Many Sandwich-area residents remember picking out matching cloth feed bags to make into garments later.

Six

HOME, FAMILY, AND LEISURE TIME

George Bark owned one of the earliest farms in the area on West Sandwich Road. The home and barn stand on the farm north of town on West Sandwich Road and are still owned by the Bark family.

South of the Bark farm toward Sandwich stands the Fraser farm, another early farm in the area. William Fraser was the first of his family to own property. The Fraser family still own and reside on the farm. The Fraser family received a special recognition from the Illinois Department of Agriculture in July 2007 for having a sesquicentennial farm.

The Adams family reunion was held in May 1887 to celebrate Augustus Adams's 81st birthday. A New York native, Adams established a machine shop in New York and later in Elgin before coming to Sandwich, where he started a machine shop that led to the formation of the Sandwich Manufacturing Company. He was a state legislator in the house and senate in the mid-1850s.

Dr. Charles Winne, an early physician, surgeon, pharmacist, and drugstore owner, is shown with his beloved granddaughter Rachel Converse. He came to Sandwich in 1866 and retired in 1888. After retiring he served as the township supervisor from 1894 to 1911.

Julius M. Hummel was well known in and around Sandwich. He was not only a businessman, but he was also the mayor. He helped start the Sandwich Opera House, the fire department, the Sandwich Fair, the Oak Ridge Cemetery, and he served on the school board. He entertained with his fiddle, and he wrote many of his newspaper advertisements in verse. He was considered by many to be a "real character."

Pliny Southwick owned this large home at 319 North Lafayette Street, shown in this 1907 photograph. The attractive stone wall surrounding the home is unique. The R. G. Seitzinger family lived here for many years.

Miles Beach Castle and his wife, Freelove, were business people in early Sandwich. Castle was founder of the Castle Bank in 1856, editor of the *Sandwich Argus* newspaper, a lumber and coal dealer, and a state senator for two terms. The Castle family is still active in the Castle Bank, formerly the Sandwich State Bank.

James Patten was a native of the Sandwich area and became a "wheat king" and a leading board of trade operator. He always remembered his hometown and was a generous benefactor for local churches, the hospital, and the Oak Mound Cemetery northwest of Sandwich.

This lovely home on North Lafayette Street was built for James and Caroline (Mosher) Warner, owners of the Warner Mercantile business in Sandwich. This photograph was taken about 1900.

Hardware merchant George Kleinsmid built the Kleinsmid mansion on West Center Street in 1871. Resembling a European castle complete with tower, the brick home has 20 rooms. It has been a single-family dwelling, an apartment house, and a place of business. The mansion is on the National Register of Historic Places.

Son of hardware merchant Kleinsmid, Rufus von Kleinsmid joined the University of Southern California staff and became its chancellor in 1946 after 25 years as university president. He visited Sandwich many times, the last being in 1963 when he was the honored guest of a dinner and reception.

Ornate fretwork adorned the interior doorways in the Frank Carpenter home on West Church Street, built in 1899. Early residents of this city, the Carpenter family built the third home in the area after the town was laid out.

Lenora Clark and her mother pose in front of their North Joles Street home about 1915. Earl and Addie Olson owned the home later.

One of Sandwich's early doctors built this large brick home in the 1850s, taking up the entire 500 block of East Third Street. The Herbert Johnson family owned the home for many years.

Latham Castle, son of Miles B. Castle, served as Illinois attorney general from 1952 to 1959. A highlight of Castle's career occurred in 1956 when he was a key figure in exposing a scandal involving the Illinois state auditor, who had embezzled state funds. Castle is pictured with the No. 7 Illinois license plate assigned to him.

David Graf was an industrial arts/diversified occupations teacher for 29 years at Sandwich. He was the National Teacher of the Year in 1968, and he was a World War II hero who was awarded a purple heart. Many students remember this quotation on his blackboard: "He who has a trade has an estate." He helped start Open Door sheltered workshop and Indian Valley Vocational School.

Bob Hope made an appearance at the Sandwich airport on July 20, 1969, to help raise funds to purchase an airplane for a New Guinea priest. Shirley Keller, shown here with Hope, was partially responsible for Hope's trip to Sandwich.

The city park between the railroad tracks and Railroad Street was flooded to provide ice-skating fun in the late 1800s. In the background is the Sandwich Opera House.

Davis Lake, located at the southwest edge of Sandwich, was a recreational area covering about 80 acres. There was no sand beach; the attraction was boating, fishing, swimming, hunting, and trapping. For many years, it was also the source of the town's ice supply. In 1912, tiles were installed to drain the lake and route the water east to the Little Rock Creek. Pictured are Edward Hennis (left) and Theodore Stinson boating on Davis Lake in 1910.

The Sandwich Fishing Club (pictured) was believed to include the Crofoot family, early residents in Sandwich.

This Sandwich Gun Club photograph was taken in June 1886, the day the club held its first shoot at Davis Lake. For the first time, members saw clay targets in flight. The initial shoot used black powder with 20 single targets at 18 yards.

A hoop drill was held in 1893 at the W. W. Woodbury School. These children wore their best clothes for the occasion.

Union Band members pose in their uniforms about 1880, the year after they organized. An 1883 newspaper article told of Henry Wilder's new coronet that was silver plated and gold tipped, one of the best ones made. The cost was nearly $60. Wilder was the only leader of the Union Band. The band appeared at local functions until it disbanded in 1926.

The Sandwich Fire Department was organized in 1884 but dates back many years before its formal organization. The men battled fires with hand-pulled carts and water supplied from three windmill-driven cisterns. Samuel Mitten was the first fire marshal. The city and rural fire departments merged in 1967.

Popular diversions of the fire department were the running team and the hose team. Starting in 1892, the teams competed all over the state, winning the championship in 1908 in Lincoln and several other times. The last running team was in 1920.

Members of the Sandwich Camp 147 of Modern Woodmen of America members are pictured in 1893. They were a fraternal-financial group that offered insurance. They did not accept miners, baseball players, or saloon keepers, among others, but did accept "low risk" members. The women's group was the Royal Neighbors of America.

Pictured about 1899, the Methodist Sunday school orchestra, from left to right, is (first row) Jennie Greenfield, Guy Wilder, Andrew Cook, Roy Scott, and Mrs. Harry Rugh; (second row) Rudy Solfisberg, Harriet Palmer, and Herbert Rohrer; (third row) Frank Carpenter, Theodore Boyd, ? Smith, and Albert Spach.

The VFW band received an invitation to play at the New York World's Fair in 1940. The fair offered to bear the expense of admission to the grounds and a place to store the band instruments.

In 1911, this may have been the local bicycle club lined up next to Frank and Emory Stockham's shop at the corner of Center and Eddy Streets. Bicycles, also referred to as "wheels," were a popular source of transportation in the early 1900s.

A car club with 25 or 30 cars went through Sandwich in August 1915, stopping for lunch and posing for this photograph at the corner of Main and Center Streets. They were on a run from Chicago to Sulphur Lick Springs near Wedron on the Starved Rock Trail.

Grocer Fred Harrod led the Woman's Literary and Study Club on a tour to a wholesale grocery facility in Chicago in 1910. The ladies dressed in their finest clothing for the Chicago trip. The group, organized in 1895, owned and managed the library and worked with the city and schools on improvements.

The first picture theater in Sandwich was the Royal Theatre operated by J. Ray Gage about 1907. It was vaudeville, and a person was hired to play piano during the show. It was located on North Main Street just north of the corner Hummel building. Later it was located at 120 East Railroad and renamed the Avalon.

The State Theatre at 120 East Railroad Street was earlier known as the Avalon and then the American Theatre. In 1933, a new owner held a contest to name the theater. Eureka was chosen; however, at the same time an opportunity arose to purchase a ready-made neon-lighted marquee with the name State. It was purchased and named the State Theatre. *The Golden Horde* was a 1951 movie. The theater closed in the mid-1960s.

While on a class picnic, members of the 1918 Sandwich senior class have fun hanging from a pole under the Little Rock Creek Bridge.

At the present site of the forest preserve on Route 34 west of Sandwich, the Sannauk Country Club was opened in 1928. This photograph shows the eighth tee at the golf course. The grounds were sold in 1937, and it became a county forest preserve in 1939.

This group of Girl and Boy Scouts posed in 1937 at Sandwich City Hall. From left to right, they are (first row) John Montgomery, Donald Armstrong, John Haskin, Dean Francis, Frederick Lindner, Oscar Puhan, Reed Larson, Robert Bistline, and Edward Easter; (second row) assistant Donald Coakes, Charles Marrs, Janet Ogilive, Max Priesman, Mayor Wallace Cochran, Howard Wissel, Joan Potter, and Ralph Moore; (third row) councilman Earl Shales, superintendent of schools Lynn G. Haskin, and city attorney Truman Crowell.

Many area people think of Nina Carr, the wife of Clarence Carr, when parades and calliopes are mentioned. Nina played this calliope, belonging to the Herbert Johnson family, for local entertainment and area parades in the late 1940s through the 1950s. From her earnings playing at the theater for silent movies in the 1920s, she purchased a new Ford Model T.

Tommy and Anne Fairclough owned and operated the Fairway Skating Palace at the east end of Sandwich on Route 34. Tommy was usually the organist. The roller rink opened with a tent in 1940, and then a new building opened that same year. It was destroyed by fire in September 1941 but was rebuilt. The Faircloughs left the business in 1952 but returned in 1962 and owned it until it closed in 1979.

Harold "Bub" Goodwick formed the Glen Victorian band in 1927 and played banjo. Later he and several young musicians formed Bub and His Boys, playing at the Baker's feed tent at the Sandwich Fair. This photograph shows them sometime between 1959 and 1961 on Peoria television. Goodwick retired in 1991, but the band continued until 1995. Shown from left to right are (first row) Jack Curran and Richard Morahan; (second row) Harold Goodwick, William Gardner, Donovan Goodwick, and James Herman.

Seven

AROUND TOWN

The first post office in Sandwich opened in 1850 at 35 East Center Street. In the fall of 1851, the postal department ordered it closed, as there was only 75¢ in receipts the previous year. It reopened after six months. For a number of years, the post office was in various businesses until it moved to its permanent home on Eddy Street.

A wagon loaded with boxes in downtown Sandwich is ready to make deliveries. The Alfred and Elmer Marselus brothers' elevator is in the background. James Patten and W. G. Beveridge purchased the elevator business from Marselus Brothers in 1898. Patten continued the business after Beveridge died in 1902. Today it is a parking lot.

On January 13, 1918, about 400 citizens from all walks of life used shovels to clear the railroad tracks from the Somonauk Creek to the Little Rock Creek. Blizzards paralyzed train traffic and coal delivery until the tracks were cleared. In appreciation, the railroad left an extra carload of coal in Sandwich.

Here is an early-1900s view on Wells Street looking north toward Railroad Street. The Wallace building with its distinctive peaked corner is on the right.

Sandwich's power plant on East Railroad Street was built in 1883. That same year, one mile of water mains was laid. The stand pipe was 12 feet in diameter and 100 feet high, and it held 84,000 gallons of water. It was removed in 1956 when a water tower was built.

This photograph, taken about 1910, shows businesses on South Main Street from Railroad Street. They are, from right to left, Sandwich State Bank, Burkhart's Bakery and Restaurant, Campbell's Saloon, Goodman's, and T. A. Weir's Hardware.

A January 19, 1916, flood damaged homes, businesses, and industry in Sandwich. Frozen ground did not allow the water to soak in. It was the worst flood since 1892 when over 200 acres of the city was underwater.

New automobiles were unloaded from a railroad car near the freight depot in 1912. There were 70 automobiles in and around the city in 1910. A 1907 law limited the speed on country roads to 20 miles per hour, on town streets to 15 miles per hour, in business districts to 10 miles per hour, and at corners to 6 miles per hour.

A picture of Railroad Street east of Eddy Street in the early 1900s shows, from right to left, the Wallace Block, Northern Illinois Utilities, Bleitz Furniture and Undertaking, the City Hotel, and the Sandwich City Hall/Opera House in the background. The foreground shows trees on the north side where there is now a parking lot.

At the southwest corner of Railroad and Main Streets in the late 1890s, the Sandwich State Bank was the corner business. From 1896 to 1899, U. S. Clothing was next door to the south.

Oak Ridge Bridge, near Sandwich, Ill.

A new Oak Ridge Bridge replaced an earlier one across the Somonauk Creek at Suydam Road west of Sandwich in 1955. The first bridge across the creek was built about 1861.

At one time, the entry to Oak Ridge Cemetery west of Sandwich on Suydam Road was covered with ivy. The cemetery was chartered in 1870 as the Union Cemetery; the name was changed in 1895 to Oak Ridge. Several parcels have been added to total the present 22.6 acres. In 1999, Sandwich Township became the owner and caretaker of the cemetery.

In 1836, Fanny Harmon was the first burial at Oak Ridge Cemetery, which was known at the time as the Harmon farm. There are now over 8,000 graves on the grounds. This photograph, taken about 1915, shows a house and windmill that are no longer there.

Enos Doan built the Grecian-style opera house/city hall for $12,000 in 1878 while Jules Hummel was mayor. Today city and opera house offices are on the lower floor, and the auditorium and balcony are on the second floor. It was renovated in 1895 and again from 1984 to 1986 after years of neglect. It was placed on the National Register of Historic Places in 1979.

On October 26, 1984, a collapse of the south exterior wall slowed restoration of the Sandwich City Hall/Opera House. City offices are in the building along with the opera house office, auditorium, reception, and community rooms.

An early photograph of the west side of Main Street between the railroad tracks and Church Street shows that many of the buildings look similar today. The brick building on the right is the Marcy Block building that was built by A. A. Marcy. Many businesses and offices have been located in the building; apartments are now on the second floor.

New sidewalks were being poured along West Center Street next to the Hummel building when this photograph was taken prior to 1920. Cement was mixed and hauled by hand for the new sidewalks.

In 1918, buildings were torn down from Main to Eddy Streets along Railroad Street to make room for this city park, which was finished in 1920. The gas station shown in the center is a parking lot today. The Eddy Street corner was the site of the early city jail and first fire house in the 1880s. Dr. A. A. Legner's veterinarian office was in part of the building in the 1930s.

In the early 1900s, Thomas Dean's harness shop, F. W. Haupt's shoe shop, and Stockholm and Son's meat market were located at the northeast corner of Main and Church Streets. These buildings have been torn down; the area is now a parking lot.

Dr. George S. Culver and Dr. Louise Culver's residence at 510 North Main Street was called Culvers' Sanitarium (above). Horatio N. and Ila Woodward bought the residence in 1921 for $8,000 and donated it to the community for the H. N. Woodward Memorial Hospital (below). It remained in operation until 1960. Today a nursing home is at the site. The first hospital in Sandwich was opened in 1915 on East Center Street by Dr. Guy Wormley and Dr. Erwin Dudley.

Sandwich
Mineral
Spring

aug 1907.

There are photographs and mention of Sandwich Mineral Springs, but the location is unknown. This was taken in 1907.

"THE GRISWOLD SPRING,"
Located on the South road
From Sandwich to Plano.

Griswold Springs was a well-known spot southeast of Sandwich on the 35-acre property of William Griswold. A pipe was installed in the springs to make it easy to get pure, clear, cold water. Griswold encouraged residents to bring their containers and take home water from the springs. A shaded picnic area allowed visitors to spend some time there. When the bridge was replaced, the springs were covered.

The present post office was built at 22 North Eddy Street in 1938. First known as Newark Station and often confused with the town of Newark, its name was changed to Sandwich in 1855. In 1930, city mail delivery began. In 1952, the post office advanced to first-class status due to the increase in receipts. In 1963, zip codes were introduced.

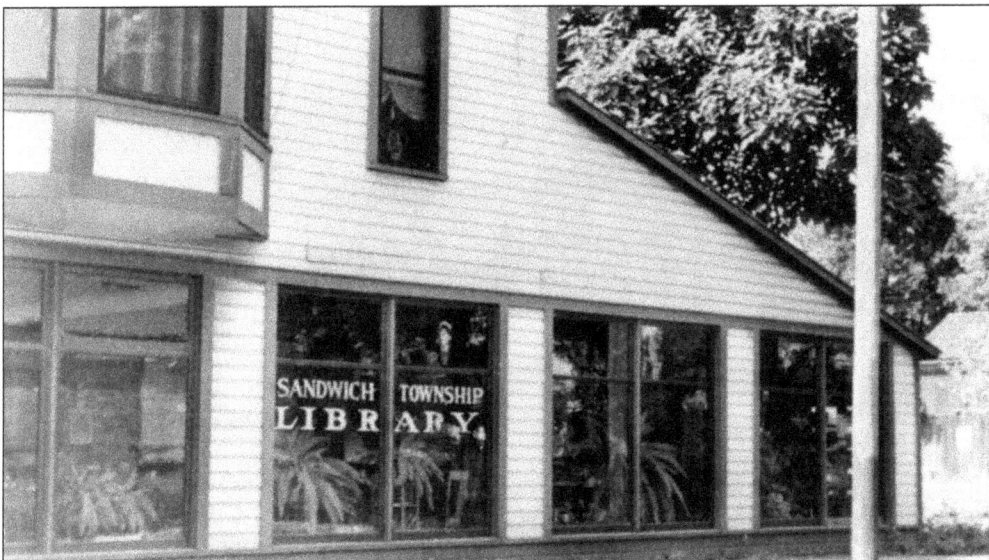

One early location of the library was on the corner of West Center and Green Streets in Frank N. King's livery and feed stable. The library used the space rent free. The library shown in the photograph was at this West Center Street location from 1930 until a fire destroyed the building in September 1940. It then moved to the second floor at 2 East Railroad Street.

SANDWICH PUBLIC LIBRARY
SANDWICH ILLINOIS

The brick library known for its stately pillars (above) was built in 1941 and 1942 for $40,000. A 1925 vote of the majority of people approved levying a tax to support the library. Its present home is the northeast corner of Eddy and Center Streets. The Westminster chimes were installed in 1954 as a memorial to all people who had made private gifts. The mezzanine was added in 1958. In 1926, Pauline Newton, previously a volunteer, was hired as librarian for $50 a month. Newton (left) and her collie, Skipper, were inseparable. The site of the first public library was above Moore's Drug Store on East Railroad Street in 1897. The library is now the Sandwich District Library.

Telephones first came to Sandwich in 1898; there were 13 telephones at that time. Dial telephones were installed in 1951. The 1967 two-story precast concrete building (below) on East Railroad Street was built for General Telephone Company around the existing 1950 building (above). The building has since been used for other purposes for a number of years. A small building on Church Street is the automated telephone building today.

In 1956, businesses in the 100 block of East Railroad Street are, from left to right, Sandwich Motors, State Theatre, Floyd's TV, and the Decorator's Mart.

This cement block building on West Railroad Street has had several uses. It was built about 1915 as a coliseum used for roller-skating, dances, and basketball. The roof trusses made basketball shooting tricky. The first Little 10 basketball tournament was held there in 1920 when rules were somewhat different from today. Later businesses at this site included O. A. Keele Implement and P. S. Lindner and Company.

Sandwich Community Hospital at the corner of Main and Pleasant Streets opened in the spring of 1960. It replaced the Woodward Memorial Hospital on the 500 block of North Main Street. Kishwaukee Hospital of DeKalb purchased it in 2002, renovated it, and renamed it Valley West Community Hospital.

The board of directors and others are pictured at the 1965 groundbreaking of the addition to Sandwich Community Hospital. From left to right are (first row) Marvin Tice, Richard L. Holland, Thomas Russell, Mary Larson, Richard C. Holland, Lucille Legner, and Thomas Davis; (second row) architect William Erickson, general contractor Paul Swedberg, and board president Zean Davis.

Ambulances and attendants at the emergency canopy at Sandwich Community Hospital are pictured. From left to right are Richard Meyer and Gregory Grandgeorge of Somonauk, James Dockendorf and Charles "Buzz" Lindholm of Plano, and Samuel Stratton and William Keeton of Sandwich.

This photograph of employees, board members, physicians, volunteers, and clergy was taken on the lawn of the hospital in 1985 during the 25th anniversary celebration of Sandwich Community Hospital.

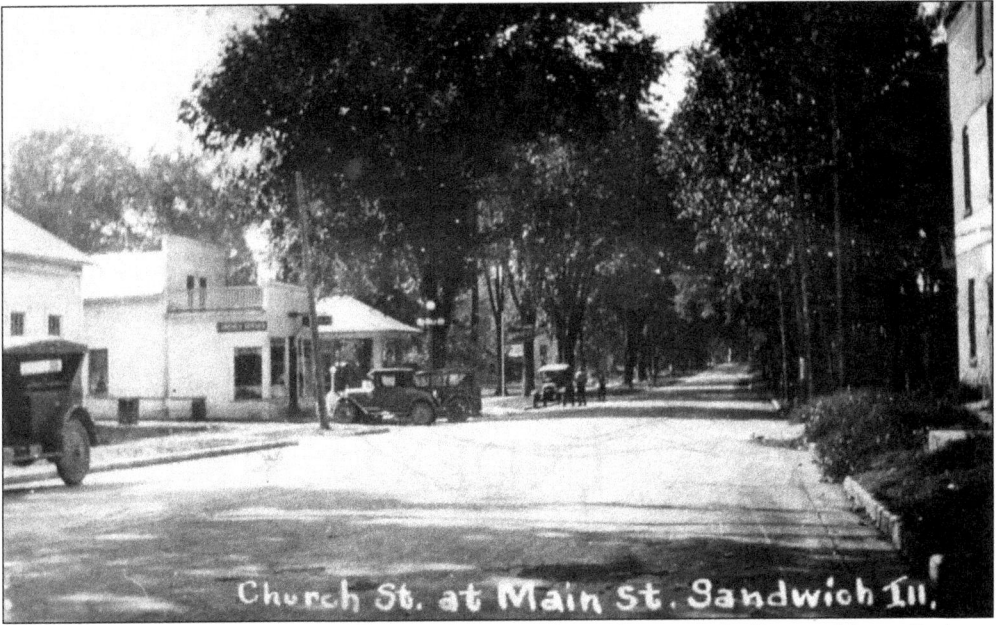

From Main Street looking west on Church Street in the early 1900s, the Pictorial Paper Package Corporation, a restaurant, and a gas station are seen on the south side of the street.

A 1909 postcard from Sandwich shows area scenes and buildings. From the upper left corner counterclockwise are Oak Ridge Cemetery entrance, a street scene looking north at Center and Main Streets, the Stone Mill and power plant, Somonauk Creek, the north side high school, the 10:20 train and railroad depot, reflections on Somonauk Creek, and a view looking south on Main Street at Railroad Street.

INDEX

Visit us at
arcadiapublishing.com

www.ingramcontent.com/pod-product-compliance
Lightning Source LLC
Chambersburg PA
CBHW050550110426
42813CB00008B/2317